Rabbits & Hares

Dr. Richard A. NeSmith

Love of Nature Series

ISSUE 14

RABBITS & HARES

Applied **P**rinciples of **E**ducation & **L**earning

APE-Learning

© 2020 Richard A. NeSmith
Love of Nature Series

MAY 2025

ISBN: 9798692783004

FLESCH-KINCAID GRADE LEVEL: 7.1

Rabbits & Hares
(Family: Leporidae)

Rabbits and hares are found throughout the world except for the very driest or very coldest regions. Fourteen rabbit and hare species are found living in North America. There are far too many species to address in a single issue, but a list of species not discussed here is provided at the end. All of these are considered *lagomorphs* (Order: Lagomorpha). This order includes two

families: **Leporidae** (hares and rabbits) and their cousins, Ochotonidae (pikas). *Lago-* means "hare" and *-morpha* means "form." We will focus on three species of these and how they are so successful in their ecosystems.

Rabbits have always been favored in American literature, especially by children and in children's stories. Various tales and folklore stories present the rabbit as the clever trickster who eventually outwits his enemy or adversary. Such is the case with Brer Rabbit, Bugs Bunny, or even Peter Rabbit.

North American rabbits and hares seem to be thriving wherever they are found. The most common ones include the **Eastern Cottontail** (Sylvilagus *floridanus*), the **Jackrabbit**, and the **Marsh Rabbit**. There are 30 species of hare (genus Lepus) and 28 species of rabbit. One of the first things we need to recognize is that the rabbit is not the same species as the hare. They are very different, and they do not interbreed. However, all of these are often endearingly referred to by people as *bunnies*.

However, this term was first used as a compliment or flattery term during the early 17th century for a person one really likes, particularly a young girl. Bunny later became a *pet* name for a rabbit or squirrel.

Very early on, rabbits were called **conies**. Even the 1611 A.D. Bible refers to these animals several times. The word *conies* is based on the French *conil*. The term *rabbit* was, at first, used to

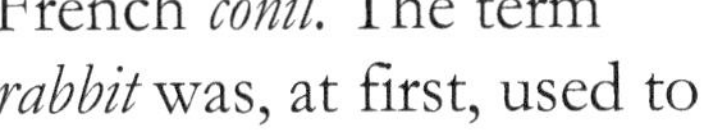
Range for the cottontail rabbit in the Americas.

refer to the young offspring of the conies. Eventually, the word took over in popularity. There is a beachside amusement park in New York called Coney Island, or *Rabbit Island*. Some believe it is one of the few references to coney left in North America. The word "hare," on the other hand, has an early old English origin, from the word *hara*, originating back to 900 AD. It means "gray."

Range

In North America, where there is vegetation, there are hares or rabbits present, including the Arctic line down into the southwestern deserts. Though the foliage is quite different in these locations, rabbits prefer soft stems, grass, or vegetables. At the same time, hares eat more hardened or dryer food such as seeds, ferns, bark and rind, buds, vegetables, small twigs, and shoots.

Rabbits and hares are incredibly successful in adapting to their environments. Though extremely shy, they seem to flourish where they live. We will learn of the many traits and behaviors that enable their success and those factors that seem to keep their population in check.

For centuries rabbits and hares were valued as food and for their fur. Domestic breeds of rabbits are still popular as

pets. Rabbits are also used for experimental purposes in various types of laboratories, including pharmaceuticals and cosmetics.

Characteristics

There are a few characteristics that rabbits and hares share in common. For example, they all are quadrupeds (four-legged), strong back legs, and can stand up on their hind legs. They have long ears, soft fur, and are prolific breeders. They are herbivores but opportunistic feeders.

Both *molt* and replace their fur, growing new coats in the spring or the fall. Summer and winter coats are different in thickness and color. Molting is when a rabbit loses its old coat. Hairs begin to shed and often can be seen out in the yard. Molting can last two to six weeks, depending on the species and the time of year. The coloration blends in very well in their environment. It provides a great deal of camouflage, keeping them reasonably undetected by would-

be predators.

Although rabbits and hares both have long incisors like rats and mice, they are not rodents. Like rats, rabbits are unable to vomit. Both rabbits and hares tend to have relatively large feet. The rabbit, however, has five toes on the front feet and four on the hind feet. The hare has four toes on each paw, with fur-covered soles leaving tracks much larger

than a rabbit. In some cultures, the rabbit's foot is carried as a charm believed to bring good luck.

Most rabbits and hares feed regularly. They will often forage or rest in groups relying on each other's eyes and ears for protection. During the heat of the day, they will rest in the shade in a hole or shallow depression under grass or bushes. Unlike the hares, the rabbits also will retreat to the burrows they may have dug. Often, woodchucks and other species built the caves or dens used by rabbits.

Both rabbits and hares are excellent swimmers, but that does not mean they prefer doing so. Some do like playing in water. This, we will see is very true of the marsh rabbit.

The similarities between rabbits and hares, however, seem to stop there. Contrary to popular belief, rabbits and hares are more different than alike. We will consider a few of these and then resort to using a modified table from research data to summarize these.

Most rabbits and hares have excellent hearing and sense of smell. These keen senses help them not only to find food but to detect and avoid predators. Their ears and nose are in constant motion, monitoring and analyzing their environment for various sounds and smells. Hares and rabbits are perhaps nature's ideal prey. Coyotes, mountain lions, bobcats, foxes, hawks, eagles, owls, and snakes will all eagerly eat them.

The ears of rabbits and hares help in two important ways: First, picking up sounds up to 1.9 miles (3 km). Their ears can be rotated 270 degrees to help hone in (focus) on a sound and revolve independently of one another, like two

separate antennae. Secondly, their ears assist in thermoregulation. Rabbits and hares do have sweat glands, but they are limited. Their sweat glands are located inside the mouth and on the paws. Panting, like a dog, is not uncommon. But the ears also act as a means of releasing body heat.

Comparison of Hares and Rabbits

Cottontail Rabbits

The most common rabbit in North America is the eastern cottontail. It received its common name from its tail, which is white underneath and is extended upwards when running. There are eight different species of cottontail rabbits in the United States and 16 in the North, Central, and South Americas, with each species inhabiting particular regions. The eastern cottontail (Sylvilagus *floridanus*) is a relatively small species that typically weighs about 2.4-3.3 lbs. (1.1-1.5 kg). Females are slightly larger than males (a trait known as *sexual dimorphism*).

The cottontail has an overlapping home range with females. Usually, a dominant female called a **doe**, will fight

other does for the best nesting site within the colony. Dominant rabbits are the most successful at breeding. Likewise, dominant males (called **bucks**) run up and down boundary lines marking their territory by depositing

droppings, scratching out shallow scrapes, or rubbing their chin in the ground, marking their area with scent from their glands. Lesser dominant-ranking rabbits do not obtain their own territory and will run off other rabbits entering another's area. But, subordinate rabbits do coexist happily with other subordinate rabbits.

Rabbits usually live in burrows, caves, or tunnels in the ground, where they prefer to stay during daylight hours. These tunnels are typically dug in well-drained soil and, often on a slope or side of a hill or mound. They try to keep hidden. A series of interconnecting rabbit tunnels are called a **warren**. The entrance holes usually have a pile of excavated soil in front of them, often covered in droppings. These tunnels can go in all directions and contain living quarters, nesting areas, and emergency exits. However, the word warren is also used to describe *a group of hares*, whereas a rabbit group is a **herd**.

Rabbits are most active at night (**nocturnal**). Most of their day is spent underground. They rest and pass their soft feces, then re-eat it a second time (discussed in the digestion section). Their consumption of these soft pellets keeps the den and living areas free of droppings. They are out and about mostly at dawn and dusk (**crepuscular**). They can, however, be spotted throughout the day during fair weather.

Hares

Hares are much larger than eastern cottontail rabbits, with the largest being the jackrabbits. Hares can reach 14 to 28 inches in length (35.6-71.1 cm) and from 3 to 12 pounds (1.3-5.4 kg) in weight. The furry coats can range from white, yellowish-brown, brown, or black-

colored and generally covered with dark markings. Hares are born with hair, and open eyes, and can even somewhat fend for themselves soon after birth.

It is easy to mistake a hare for a rabbit, particularly at a distance. Distinguishing marks are the hare's longer black-tipped ears and longer, more muscular hind legs. As a result, hares can leap up to 10 feet and run speeds of 35-40 mph (56.3-64.4 km), rising up on their toes to run.

Hares are not as sociable as their rabbit cousins. Hares are generally solitary creatures but may come together during late winter and for courting purposes. The eastern cottontail, also, is more like a hare in this matter, preferring solitary living.

Physically, hares have longer ears, larger feet, and very strong hind legs. They also have black markings on their fur. Hares also tend to be larger than rabbits. While rabbits' fur stays the same color year-round, hares change color

from brown or gray in the summer to white in the winter.

Hares live above ground. They tend to make their homes in hollow logs or a simple nest by trampling down tall grass or vegetation. And hares are faster runners, making sense since they live in open spaces, like prairies, and need the speed to outrun predators.

Jackrabbits

Jackrabbits (Lepus *californicus*) are true hares, but they are distinguished enough to mention them separately. There are five different species of jackrabbits found in North America. Jackrabbits were named for their ears. It is said that the author and humorist Mark Twain included them in a Western adventure book. He called them Jackass Rabbits, for they had the ears of a jackass (mule). Later the name was simplified to just *jackrabbit*.

One of the better-known and most widely dispersed is the Black-tail Jackrabbit. These are large, sometimes huge, up

to 24 inches (61 cm) in length, and up to 7 lbs. (3.2 kg). A black-tailed jackrabbit can live upwards of five years. They are found in the western half of the U.S., from Baja south into Mexico. They tend to favor the desert scrubland, prairies, farmlands, and dunes. If there are suitable habitats, they will move into suburban and urban areas. They adapt well to such environments. They obtain most of the needed water from the plants they eat and the required nutrition from the twice-consumed plant matter.

They forage at night and then rest in shallow holes or crevices during the day. If alarmed, they will lie motionless on the ground with their ears positioned low on their back to hide from predators. If they sense danger, they can leap up to 20 feet (6.1 m) and reach sustained speeds even in a zigzag pattern of 30+ miles per hour (48+ kph).

Diet

Though similar in appearance, the rabbit and the hares

have different types of diets. Rabbits prefer grasses and vegetables with leafy tops, such as carrots. Hares enjoy tougher, harder substances like plant shoots, twigs, and bark.

Cottontails are believed to have an astonishing 17,000 taste buds! That is nearly twice the number of taste buds humans have (8,000 to 10,000). So it is imaginable that their spectrum of taste far exceeds our own. They sense more out of vegetables and greens than we ever could appreciate. Apart from garden and lawn greens, rabbits like fruits and have no reservations about enjoying a gourmet birdseed buffet.

Unlike rodents, lagomorphs possess a second set of incisors, though this is not easily noticed as such. Both rabbits and hares have 28 teeth that continuously grow. There are six incisors. This includes two pairs of incisors on the "top" or maxilla (the second pair, often referred to as "peg teeth," are much smaller and are positioned behind the longer front incisors), and a couple of lower incisors on the jaw (mandible).

We hinted about rabbits re-eating their feces earlier. There is a reason for this. Rabbits and hares have unique digestive systems. The mammalian stomach cannot digest **cellulose**, a complex **polysaccharide**. But, herbivores have the means to digest by microbes in the gut, which can break down those complex molecules, releasing **glucose**. The grass and other plants are eaten. The rabbit or hare chews on these, starting the digestive process by mixing the food

(called a *bolus*) with amylase from the saliva. The grass or plants eaten by the Lagomorphs move from the stomach through the small intestines. Only vitamins and some macromolecules are digested at this point. Indigestible fiber leaves the small intestines and enters the **cecum**. This organ is a blind pouch, much like the human appendix, and

located in the same area. *The cecum is the most crucial part of the digestive system.* It holds ten times the amount of food the stomach can hold. It is here that the bacteria work on breaking down the cellulose. This form of digestion is referred to as **hind-gut fermentation**.

Present living in the cecum is a massive quantity of bacteria and microorganisms. These organisms live, metabolize, and reproduce here, as this is their home. The fibers will stay here for a while. As the bacteria break down the nutrients, glucose, and proteins are formed and then cross the cecum membrane and enter the rabbit or hare's blood system, where nutrients are then taken to every cell in the body. However, the percentage of nutrients from the fiber is meager. This lack of nutrition causes the rabbit to pass these fecal pellet excrement (poop) and then eat them again! So, the rabbit or hare is consuming their own feces to finish the digestion process all over again. The second passing of the predigested food is more efficient and completes the process.

Hares, including jackrabbits, eat grasses and **forbs** (flowering plants) in spring and summer. They also eat buds, twigs, and the bark of woody shrubs in winter. If given the opportunity, they can play havoc on farmer's crops, especially alfalfa fields and vegetable gardens.

Marsh Rabbits

The marsh rabbit (Sylvilagus *palustris*) is a small cottontail rabbit. It lives in marshes and swamps of coastal regions of the Eastern and Southern United States (from Virginia, along the eastern seaboard to northern sections of Florida, and through the Gulf Coast into Mobile Bay, Alabama). It

is found near regions of water and seldom found more than 40 miles from the coast. It is an excellent swimmer and will often dive underwater to escape from predators. It is similar in appearance to the eastern cottontail but has smaller ears, legs, and tails.

Marsh rabbits have reddish-brown or dark-brown fur and dark bellies. They have small, grayish tails that are dark underneath. They have short, rounded ears. Unlike the other rabbits, their feet are small, with long toenails on the hind feet. Marsh rabbits grow 14 to 16 inches in length.

Marsh rabbit's diet consists of aquatic plants, including cattails, duck potatoes, water hyacinths, and marsh grasses. They also like woody plants such as blackberry, greenbrier, and tree bark.

They are prolific breeders and do so several times between

February and September. Females may produce four litters of two to four young each year. Nests are built of fur and grass within sedges at the edge of the water. Gestation lasts 30 to 37 days.

Habitat

Rabbits can live almost anywhere. The actual habitat is

closely linked to the species and, of course, their range. Eastern cottontail rabbits prefer heavy brush, treed forests with open areas nearby, edges of swamps, and weed patches. The marsh rabbit is a small cottontail found in marshes and swamps of coastal regions of the Eastern and Southern United States. As we have seen, Marsh rabbits prefer bottomlands, swamps, wetlands, and hammocks, and they are outstanding swimmers. Hammocks are little islands of trees growing up on soil several inches above the waterline, so are surrounded by wetlands or on slopes between wetlands and uplands. The jackrabbit favors open prairies and sparsely vegetated deserts.

Rabbits can dig burrows. Their natural habitats include woods, meadows, forests, farmland, grassland, moorlands, salt marshes, embankments, sand dunes, and even cliffs. Hares are found in more arid ecosystems. Jackrabbits can be seen from sea level elevations up to 10,000 feet (3,000 m).

The eastern cottontail lives in the eastern and south-central United States, southern Canada, and eastern Mexico. They can also be found in Central America and northernmost South America. This rabbit prefers meadows (grasslands, similar to a field or pasture) and shrubby areas.

Some rabbits are relatively social and often live in **colonies**, with up to 20 other individuals. Other species are not so

social. The social ones need the companionship of their own kind. Hares, however, are not social and are very much **solitary**. Rabbits and hares do not mix, nor do they

interbreed. But, rabbits rarely live alone, and a single rabbit is an unhappy rabbit.

Behavior

Rabbits can die from stress-induced heart attacks. A predator can scare a rabbit to death. One reason may be that the rabbit's heart rate is already very high by comparison with other mammals. Their resting heart rate is between 140 and 180 beats a minute. When the heart rate goes beyond 180, very little blood is being moved through the body. Lack of blood means a lack of oxygen to the brain and other cells. Another cause of a rabbit's sudden death is an infection from a rabbit **calicivirus**, which can

also be found in cats.

Also, getting wet becomes a problem because wet rabbit fur takes a long time to dry. If left wet, the rabbit can quickly get **hypothermia**, even on warm days. Hypothermia is when the body loses heat faster than it can produce heat. This drop in temperature leads to shock, and body organs stop functioning.

No species of rabbit or hare hibernates. They endure the winter weather face-on. Finding enough food and water is a problem. During such times, they will venture out during the daylight hours to forage despite the risk. Some of the vast northern ones will develop snow-white coats, but that is not true for all. A frigid day can lead them to look for older dens for coverage and warmth.

Reproduction

For the hares, mating season occurs during spring and fall. For rabbits, they breed throughout the spring and summer months.[1] Usually, two litters are produced per year, upon which two to four baby rabbits are born. During the breeding season, male rabbits and hares, respectively, will fend off or fight other males to establish dominance by using their front paws, much like a boxing match. However, some of these fights involve females rejecting some of the males' advances. Because of the numbers and

bizarre sights, some have called this time *March madness*. This behavior explains the common phrase, "mad as a March hare."

---

[1] A doe rabbit can bear one to four litters (usually three), a year, with one to four leverets per litter.

For hares, pregnancy lasts 42 days and ends with six babies known as **leverets**. These little ones are ***precocial,*** meaning they are born with their eyes open and fully furred. Therefore, they don't require parental care and can run, leap, and play shortly after birth.

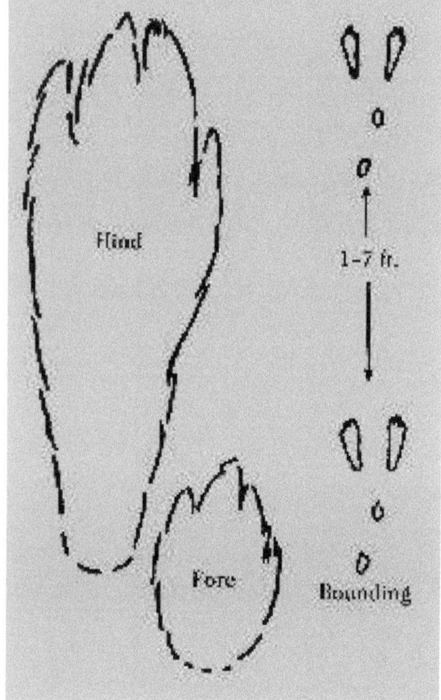

However, Rabbits will have a gestation period from 27 to 42 days, depending on the species. Their infants, called **kits, kittens,** or **bunnies**, are born naked, blind, and helpless, which is why it's smart for them to live in more secure dens underground. For both rabbits and hares, mothers leave the nest to find food and return to nurse the babies after dusk and before dawn. Leverets are weaned at four weeks, and bunnies are between four to eight weeks of age.

The mortality rate for hares and rabbits is less than 10%. However, it may reach 50% or even 100% during the first two weeks of the newborn's life. However, the mortality rate of four to eight-week-old rabbits remains high. It then decreases to near zero in rabbits aged three months or older.

Hares in the wild can live to 9 years of age. Wild rabbits, however, live for less than one year. Arctic hares have a lifespan of about 18 months.

Because the rabbit and hare are indeed very different from one another, a table has been created for the *want-to-know*

readers. Here we summarized the similarities and the differences.

RABBITS & HARES

COMPARISON OF A RABBIT TO A HARE (INCLUDING A JACKRABBIT) [2]

Similarities

1. Rabbits and hares have short tails.

2. Both have a split lip (harelip), although there are slight differences.

3. Both are prey animals that must rely on hiding or running to evade predators.

4. Both breed prolifically, bearing four to eight litters each year, depending on the species.

5. Game for hunters for food and fur, pests to farmers and gardeners due to crop destruction.

Differences between Rabbits and Hares
Different physical features and lifestyles.
Hares are generally larger and faster than rabbits.
Hares have longer ears and larger feet than rabbits.
Hares have very long and more muscular hind legs than rabbits.
Hares have black markings on their fur.
Rabbits are altricial (their young are born blind and hairless). Hares are precocial (their young are born with hair and can see). Young hares can fend for themselves very quickly after birth.
A young hare is called a leveret, and a young rabbit is called a kitten or bunny.
Both molt and then grow new hair in spring and fall, respectively. • Rabbits' brown summer fur is replaced with grayer fur. • Hares, especially those living in snowy regions, turn white in

---

[2] Table modified from data provided by: Thibedi, L. (2008). Imvubu 20:2, 6. The Amathole Museum.

the winter.

Hunters say that a hare has a much gamier flavor than a rabbit, which tastes similar to chicken.

Hares have not been domesticated, while rabbits are often kept as pets.

All rabbits, except the cottontail rabbit, live underground in burrows or warrens. In contrast, hares live in nests above ground, as does the cottontail rabbit.

Hares rely on running, rather than burrowing, for protection.

Rabbits are very social animals and live in colonies.

Male rabbits even fight in the group for dominance. The dominant male rabbit then mates with most of the females.

By contrast, hares have a *solitary* life. They pair off only for mating, with almost no fighting among them.

Rabbits have five toes on the front feet and four on the hind feet. Hares have four toes on each paw with fur-covered soles leaving larger tracks.

Rabbits prefer soft stems, grass, or vegetables; hares eat harder food, such as barks, rinds, buds, small twigs, and shoots.

Hares have larger bodies and longer ears.

There are over 305 breeds of domestic rabbits in 70 countries around the world.

.Miscellaneous

Most rabbits and hares in the warmer regions carry **tularemia**, "rabbit fever," or "deer fever." Tularemia is a rare infectious disease caused by the bacterium Francisella *tularensis*. In humans, it attacks the skin, eyes, lymph nodes,

and lungs. It can be transmitted through an infected tick, deerfly, or other insects. It can also be contracted from handling infected animal carcasses, eating contaminated food, drinking contaminated water, or breathing in the bacteria.

Prevention of tularemia infection includes using a high-grade insect repellant. If handling rabbits or hares, wash one's hands carefully. When cooking, always cook the meat thoroughly, but *an infected rabbit should be discarded and not eaten*. Though many mammals are susceptible to rabies, rabbits, and hares are rarely infected with it. Neither have they been known to transmit rabies to humans.

Another factor that rabbits and other mammals encounter is that of **botflies** and bot-fly **larvae**. Several species of flies (warble flies, heel flies, and gadflies) lay their larvae directly on the animal's fur. The larvae then burrow into the skin, just under the epidermis. There it becomes an internal parasite living on the rabbit's flesh and blood. This larva is called a "bot" from the word meaning *maggot*.

So, in reality, this maggot will then feed and grow in the host's flesh (and some species within the gut). Once it reaches maturity, it will eat its way back out of the skin and drop to the ground, where it *metamorphoses* into a **pupa** (the stage right before adulthood). As an adult fly, it will then seek a host for its eggs. One species can parasitize humans. Notice the photograph (see page 36) of the embedded

Looking at this rabbit's chest, one can see the botfly larva embedded under the skin.

botfly larva in the chest of the cute rabbit.

Both rabbits and hares tend to face many of the same predators and are popular targets. Predators include birds of prey (owls, hawks, and eagles), wild and domesticated dogs, cats, foxes, lynx, wolves, and humans. From the

photographs, even predation by an overly confident and aggressive blue heron is possible! (See photos on pages 25 and 26).

Night-active animals have eyes that are rich in rod cells. Nocturnal animals have a mirror-like membrane at the back of their eyes behind the retina that reflects light back out the eye. The reflected light is basically unused light not absorbed by the retina. Humans do not have this membrane. The "red-eye" from a camera flash is the light reflecting off blood vessels and red tissue in our eyes.

Eyeshine is a way to describe the light reflecting in the night from an animal's eye. It is a visible effect of the tapetum lucidum, causing the pupil to appear to glow when a light is shone into the eye. If you shine a light into the rabbit's eyes, the eyeshine will be red or orange.

Rabbits and hares are both members of the Lagomorph family. They resemble one another but are different in many ways. They share some characteristics. They have very different lifestyles, eat different foods, have different habits, prefer different habitats, and even their lifespan is vastly different. Their homes are different, and the development of their offspring is very different. Yet, we endearingly call them all *bunnies.* Watching bunnies is a pastime that many people still enjoy. They seem cute, fuzzy, and friendly. They seldom cause us any harm or mishap. They are a part of nature, and all generally welcome their presence.

OTHER NORTH AMERICAN RABBITS

Pygmy Rabbit (Brachylagus *idahoensis*)

Snowshoe Hare (Lepus *americanus*)

Arctic Hare (Lepus *arcticus*)

Alaskan Hare (Lepus *othus*)

White-tailed Jackrabbit (Lepus *townsendii*)

Swamp Rabbit (Sylvilagus *aquaticus*)

Desert Cottontail (Sylvilagus *audubonii*)

Brush Rabbit (Sylvilagus *bachmani*)

Mountain Cottontail (Sylvilagus *nuttallii*)

Appalachian Cottontail (Sylvilagus *obscurus*)

New England Cottontail (Sylvilagus *transitionalis*)

REVIEW

1. Where do rabbits live in North America?

2. Where do hares live in North America?

3. List three things that rabbits and hares have in common.

4. List three things that are very different in rabbits and hares.

5. What bacterial diseases are rabbits and hares susceptible?

6. Of the rabbits and hares you read about, which have the longest lifespan? Why do you think that one might live the longest?

7. What is meant by "mad as a March hare"?

8. Which of the Lagomorphs live underground?

9. What is hypothermia, and what does it have to do with rabbits or hares?

10. What is molting? How does it benefit a rabbit or hare?

BLACK-TAIL JACKRABBIT

COLORING PAGE

http://www.supercoloring.com/coloring-pages/black-tailed-jackrabbit

Name:_______________________

Rabbits & Hares

Carefully read each statement or clue. Fill in the correct letters according to whether across or down. Use the "word bank" if needed.

Created using the Crossword Maker on TheTeachersCorner.net

molt   cecum   herbivores   marsh   hare   fermentation   botfly   bunnies   hibernate

glucose   burrow   cottontail   jackrabbit   breeding

Across

4. Dominant rabbits are the most successful at ______.
5. Pouch similar to human appendix; home to bacteria.
8. How Lagomorphs are able to get nutrition from plants: as hind-gut ___________.
12. Can lay an egg that becomes an internal parasite?
13. What no Lagomorph does in the wintertime.
14. Possibly the most known and common rabbit?

Down

1. Rabbits' place during the resting or sleeping?
2. Description of type of food rabbits & hares eat?
3. Not a very sociable Lagomorph.
6. This rabbit stays within 30 miles of the shoreline.
7. Possibly has the longest ears of all?
9. Endearing name used to a young girls or ladies?
10. Chickens lose their feather but rabbits and hares lose their fur.
11. Carbohydrate fuel needed in each cell to sustain life.

INTERESTING SOURCES TO CONSIDER

Arctic Hare. Available at: https://youtu.be/hfkS0AzGbXI

Black-tailed Jackrabbits, the Curious Creatures of the American West. Available at: https://www.livescience.com/62742-photos-black-tailed-jackrabbits.html

Eastern Cottontail -- Sylvilagus *floridanus*. Nature Works. Available at: https://nhpbs.org/natureworks/easterncottontail.htm

Fun Facts About Cottontail Rabbits. Available at: https://youtu.be/n-GnaO7Pd9s

Hares & Rabbits: Similarities and Differences. Amathole Museum. Available at: https://bit.ly/2EKA7CT

Hares Play Hard To Get. Animal All-Stars. Available at: https://youtu.be/xCK2XIHwcvM

Hares Play Hard To Get. Animal All-Stars. Available at: https://youtu.be/xCK2XIHwcvM

Interesting facts about cottontail rabbit by weird square. Available at: https://youtu.be/6qqAv3YIqTI

Lagomorphs Rabbits And Hares Of North America. Available at: https://science.jrank.org/pages/3785/Lagomorphs-Rabbits-hares-North-America.html

Life style of wild rabbits. Bunnies Documentary. Available at: https://youtu.be/amaPA6ulwaM

North American Mammals - Rabbits, Hares, Pikas. Available at: https://www.wildlifenorthamerica.com/wildlife/Mammal/Rabbits,Hares,Pikas.html

Rabbit Documentary. National Geographic - Wildlife Animal Planet - Wild Discovery Channel. Available at: https://youtu.be/4882pmGS_H4

The Burrowers: Animals Underground - Baby Rabbits. Wildlife Documentary. Available at: https://youtu.be/U5g7x8SVgE8

The Difference Between Wild & Domestic Rabbits! Available at: https://youtu.be/wSVFq-SE4vg

The Irish Hare: A Legend In Peril. Available at: https://youtu.be/eBYcPieP9TM

This Is Why the Childhood of Rabbits Is so Terrible. Available at: https://youtu.be/In2f9-JQNqs

Wild Baby Bunnies. Available at: https://youtu.be/n-UyGqHCPWU

Wild Rabbits. Available at: https://bit.ly/33j6Zfa

ABOUT THE AUTHOR

Richard NeSmith is a native of Florida, USA. He grew up wading through the swamps of central Florida with his two younger brothers during the pre-Disney era, and unknowingly, falling in love with biology, wildlife, and nature. He has lived in seven American states, twice in Australia, and once in Mexico City. He holds eight university degrees and has taught for 14 years in secondary schools, here and abroad, and another 13 years as a professor in several American universities. His service includes professor of science education, Dean of Education, Campus Dean, as well as an online instructor. His passion for learning (and *how we learn*) did not develop until *after* graduating from high school. His only explanation for this is that *having a goal made all the difference in the world*. He enjoys reading, hiking, nature photography, golf, and tennis.

http://richardnesmith.obior.cc

Applied **P**rinciples of **E**ducation & Learning *presents*

APE-Learning

AMAZON AUTHOR's PAGE:

https://www.amazon.com/author/richardnesmith

Educational, wildlife, and naturalist books
Dr. Richard NeSmith.

Issue 1
Raccoons:
Friendly Bandits
Dr. Richard NeSmith

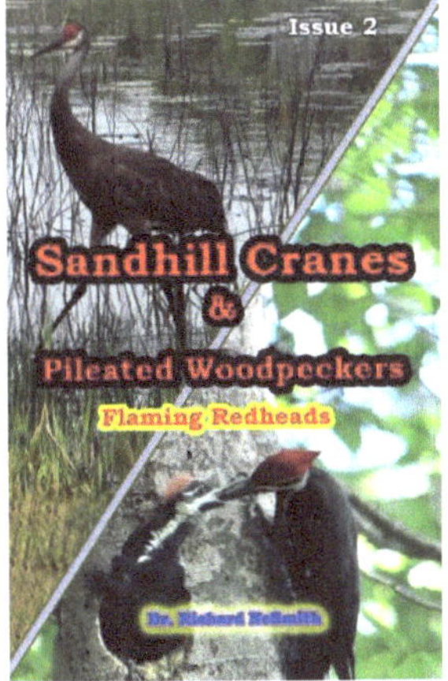
Issue 2
Sandhill Cranes
&
Pileated Woodpeckers
Flaming Redheads
Dr. Richard NeSmith

Issue 3
American
Alligators
&
Crocodiles
Dr. Richard NeSmith

Issue 4
Bobcats:
Ghostly Elusive
Dr. Richard NeSmith

Issue 5
Foxes:
Sneaky Rascals
Dr. Richard NeSmith

Issue 6
Armadillo:
Little Armored One
Dr. Richard NeSmith

Issue 7
Squirrels:
Bushy Tail Scampers
Dr. Richard NeSmith

Issue 8
River Otters:
Aquatic Clowns!
Dr. Richard NeSmith

Issue 9
Beavers:
Nature's Engineers!
Dr. Richard NeSmith

Issue 10
Black Bears
Titans of the Forest
Dr. Richard NeSmith

Issue 11
Freshwater
Turtles
Dr. Richard NeSmith

Issue 12
FUNGI, LICHENS
& MUSHROOMS
Dr. Richard NeSmith

Paperbacks:
http://amazon.com/author/richardnesmith

e-books: https://bit.ly/3iuCgB3

[i] Special thanks to the following who kindly provided permission to use their photographs.

From Unsplash: Christopher Paul, Sarah Madaio, Fidel Fernando, Vincent van Zalinge, Joshua J. Cotton, and aswathy.

From Pixabay: Joshua Choate, Mabel Amber, Lubos Houska, Skeeze, Capri23auto, Thomas Drescher, Robert C., and Наталья Коллегова.

Special thanks to likeminded friends who love wildlife and who willingly shared their wonderful photos: **Cindy Frasier**, **Stacey Diamond**, **Greg Jowers**, **DS Damm**, **Karen Devens**, **Sherri Hardman**, and **Dr. Laurie Aleixo.**

Thank you to **Amathole Museum** for the use of their illustration comparing rabbits with hares (Skinner, J. D and Smithers, R. H. N. 1990. The Mammals of the Southern African Subregion. 2nd Edition. University of Pretoria). And to **Nature Works** for the use of their US cottontail distribution map. Both of these contributors are noted in the Resource page.

Thank you all!